Vicki Lansky's

practical parenting

TOILET TRAINING

BANTAM BOOKS

TORONTO • NEW YORK • LONDON • SYDNEY • AUCKLAND

Thanks to—

Editors: Toni Burbank, Kathryn Ring, Sandra L. Whelan, Jean-Marie Sohlden

Consultants:
Karen Olness, M.D., Minneapolis Children's Health Center
Judy Owens-Stively, M.D., Minneapolis Children's Health Center
Peggy Osterholm, R.N., P.N.P., Wayzata Children's Clinic
Rebecca Kajander, R.N., P.N.P., Wayzata Children's Clinic
Burton White, Ph.D., Center for Parent Education, Newton, Mass.
Joan Reivich, Booth Maternity Center, Philadelphia

Illustrator: Jack Lindstrom

Special thanks to the parents who shared their words and feelings. Their quotes are reprinted with permission from Vicki Lansky's *Practical Parenting* newsletter.

TOILET TRAINING
A Bantam Book / August 1984

Library of Congress Cataloging in Publication Data

Lansky, Vicki.
    Toilet training.

    (Vicki Lansky's Practical parenting)

    1. Toilet training. I. Title. II. Series: Lansky,
Vicki. Practical parenting.
HQ770.5.L36 1984   649'.62   83-46006
ISBN 0-553-34070-0

Published simultaneously in the United States and Canada

Contents

Introduction

Why Is Toilet Training Such a Big Deal?

A number of things can contribute to a parent's strong need to get a child toilet trained, *right now*. Some are pressures from your peers, fear that you're failing as a parent by tolerating a child in diapers, the enrollment of your child in nursery school, and, not least, the strains and stresses of what's known as "diaper drag."

First, assume that any neighbor or relative who claims victory in toilet training her child before yours is lying (well, exaggerating), fantasizing, or redefining the term. I never considered my children really trained till they could get in and out of the bathroom, get their clothes off and back on, clean their bottoms properly, and wash their hands all without any help from me. But for now, we'll work with that more limited but still important definition that simply has the child saying, "Get me to the potty" in time.

Second, plan not to take it personally. Your child's readiness for toilet training is no indication of his or her IQ, your level of parenting ability, or your parents' attempts to raise you properly. (Despite what your mother-in-law might say, your 3-year-old still being in diapers will not affect her social status.)

Third, be assured that it will happen. When your child is truly ready, physically and emotionally, toilet training will happen—rapidly. And be assured also that while it's going on, toilet training is very important, but when it's accomplished, you'll wonder why it seemed like such a big deal!

Fourth, remember that you are not alone. When your child regresses for the third time, meditate on the fact that, simultaneously, several million other mothers and fathers are earning their toilet-training merit badges, too.

Perhaps the biggest controversy on this subject today is the language used to describe the process. It's called "toilet learning," "potty training," "toilet teaching," and "toileting." Yes, *learning* may be more accurate than *training*, at least according to today's wisdom, but I've never had anyone ask me if my child was toilet learned. So please bear with my preference for toilet training, and don't search for deeper meanings.

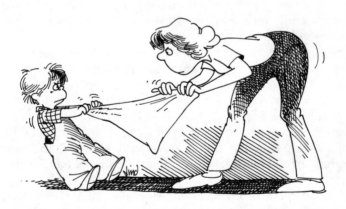

Remember that there are three things you can never make your child do—eat, sleep, or go to the bathroom.

1

When Is My Child Ready to Be Toilet Trained?

The days of hand-hemmed, hand-washed, line-dried diapers are gone, thank goodness. So that should signal an era of more relaxed, less anxious parents, right?

Wrong!

The prospect of toilet training in the 1980s evokes as much concern as it ever did. The pressures of friends and relatives—even doctors—as well as practical considerations have pushed many parents into premature toilet-training attempts that eventually end in failure and frustration.

It is true that current wisdom has made many parents less intense about having a child trained before the age of 2. Early training is no longer the norm, but once a parent decides that the time has come, relaxation seems to go out the window.

The simple fact is that your child must be physically and emotionally mature enough to understand and to control what is happening in the process. If you begin to toilet train a child before this point, the odds are that it simply won't work. A child who is "trained" before age 2 usually has a toilet-trained parent—one who is trained to catch the child!

Physical maturation first becomes possible with voluntary

control over the sphincter muscles—which means being able to open and close very specific internal muscles. While this is possible by about 1½ years, this voluntary control only truly begins when a child can distinguish the sensations that *precede* a bowel movement or urination. This, in turn, depends on a certain amount of maturity of the central nervous system, over which no one has control.

> **You don't toilet train children—you wait for their bodies to mature (a fact God has already worked out). I made a game of it, with a timer set for 15 minutes after drinking a liquid. My son loved it!**
> *Linda Hurstell, Vicksburg, MS*

Emotional readiness is also crucial. A child's sense of self starts to emerge around the age of 2. For the first time, the child realizes that he or she can affect the world and his or her own life. Unfortunately, one of the first manifestations of this newfound power is the terrible twos stage, during which the child seems interested only in affecting his or her world negatively! It's not all bad, though. One of the positive results of this emerging assertiveness is a desire to grow up. And one of the best examples of grown-up behavior a child can relate to is being toilet trained. Once your child arrives at this point, he or she is more likely to cooperate with your toilet training efforts because he or she wants to. Body mastery is more self-rewarding than a desire to please.

The *average* child cannot be successfully toilet trained before the age of about 30 months. While girls are often trained by 2, boys may not be trained before 3 or later. But of course the exception to prove this rule will inevitably be your neighbor's child, a child in your child's play group, or your sister-in-law's child.

And no two children, even siblings who have been treated in exactly the same way, will be ready at the same age. There is a right time to begin this process, but it varies from child to child. Any time before the age of 4 is normal, despite what Grandma (or anyone else) says.

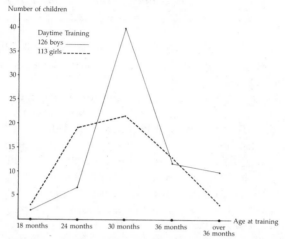

Results of a Practical Parenting Newsletter survey. It's true—girls are generally trained earlier than boys!

You might wish to consider the advantages and disadvantages of early toilet training before making a decision to try it. By early, I mean at age 1½–2.

Advantages of Early Toilet Training

The advantages of early toilet training are obvious. In fact, they're the same as the advantages for toilet training in general, you just get to enjoy them sooner. Parents are anxious to have their children trained for a variety of reasons. Caring for an untrained child takes more planning and a lot of equipment. Travel and baby-sitting are more cumbersome. Wet dia-

> As one who did not get trained until age 4½ myself, I would *not* suggest the issue first. Once either of ours decided he/she wanted to use the potty and wear panties, *that* was the key.
>
> *Jodi Junge, Huntingdon Valley, PA*

pers can cause diaper rash. (One mother told me her daughter trained herself in one day to escape a particularly painful case of diaper rash.)

On the average, dealing with diapers consumes approximately ten hours a week for most parents. A year's worth of disposable diapers costs several hundred dollars; a diaper service costs about the same. Cloth diapers are not as cheap as they would seem at first, when you consider the cost of detergent, electricity, and wear and tear on the laundry equipment, not to mention Mom and Dad. Some nursery schools won't take children in diapers, or they may charge more for the inconvenience. All in all, life is a lot more pleasant and less complicated when diapers become a thing of the past. And the attitude of most parents is "the sooner the better."

> Just as we were finished toilet training our son, our next child (a girl) started wanting to use the toilet. She would watch her brother sit on the toilet and cry to take her diaper off. I fought her for three weeks, refusing to potty train two at once. But finally I thought if she was that insistent, she was ready. I put her in training pants, and three weeks later (at 18 months) she was completely trained.
>
> *Charlotte Martin, Bartlesville, OK*

Disadvantages of Trying to Toilet Train Too Early

However nice it is to finally have a toilet-trained child, the process shouldn't (and usually can't) be rushed into. Consider these disadvantages:

- Trying to toilet train a child who isn't ready can prove to be futile and a waste of time.

- A child who is forced to try to comply may experience an extreme sense of failure (and so may the parents!).

- Premature toilet training may create a war of wills in which no one wins. A child may actually hold back bowel movements, creating serious constipation, in an attempt to control the parent.

- The stresses of futile attempts at training may cause a parent to use inappropriate regimentation or force. Studies show that one of the principal causes of child abuse is parental frustration over a child's unsuccessful toilet training.

- A child's anxiety about toilet training may lead to bedwetting into adulthood. (A study of 18-year-old British army inductees provided a classic example of this. Fifteen percent were still bed-wetters after having been "toilet trained" before the age of one.)

I have been at odds with my 4-year-old for more than two years. We seem to backslide a lot (sort of like two steps forward, one step back). I think I put too much pressure on him in the beginning. We are trying to be more laid back with our younger child.

Becky Wilkins, Lubbock, TX

What Are the Basics?

You'll probably think about toilet training long before you get into it. One thing you'll want to do is settle any major differences of opinion between you and your spouse (or anyone else who will be involved) about methods and ways of handling things. Some compromise may be called for, because basic consistency is very important. But there should be total agreement that there's no place for punishment in any phase of toilet training.

General Signs of Readiness

From the time your child is about 2 (though it may be nearer 3 for some), you should watch for signs of readiness for training. If certain signs are clearly present, and the child is basically past the negative "no-to-every-request" stage, he or she is probably ready. You'll know your child is ready when he or she:

- Is aware of the "need to go," and shows it by facial expression or by telling you.

- Can express and understand one-word statements, including such words as "wet," "dry," "potty," and "go."

- Demonstrates imitative behavior.

- Dislikes wet or dirty diapers. (Don't confuse this with *your* level of discomfort or inconvenience.)

- Is able to stay dry for at least two hours or wakes up dry in the morning or after a nap.

- Is able to pull pants up and down.

- Is anxious to please you.

- Has a sense of social "appropriateness" (wet pants can be an embarassment).

- Tells you he or she is *about* to go. (Praise such statements to set the stage for a child who wishes to please you by learning to use the toilet or potty.)

- Asks to use the potty chair or toilet.

Check Fluid Intake

If your child shows all the signs of readiness except the ability to stay dry for at least two hours, check fluid intake. Any child who is drinking milk, water, or fruit juices continuously cannot stay dry for long. Also, check with your doctor about the possibility of lactose intolerance (an inability to digest milk properly), which can result in cramps, loose stools, and the inability to hold a bowel movement for more than a moment.

Some Preparatory Steps

There is much to be said for setting the stage well before you begin toilet training. Few children train themselves. They need and deserve help and guidance. A child who has become familiar with bathroom procedures and equipment is more likely to become trained quickly and easily than one who has not.

- Take your child into the bathroom with you. It's especially helpful if fathers and brothers set the example for boys, and mothers and sisters set the example for girls. Siblings are often pleased to act as role models. If your privacy is important to you, don't forget that there are neighborhood children who would probably be delighted to demonstrate.

- Try to help your child recognize the sensations of "being wet," "wetting now," and "about to be wet." Comment on signs you notice, such as the child's pausing in play or walking as if he or she is uncomfortable after elimination. Use statements such as, "You are having a BM," rather than asking the general question, "What are you doing?" Asking your child to let you know when the diaper is wet or messy is another way of increasing awareness.

- Let your child go nude in appropriate settings to help the child "see" what he or she is doing, and to help make the mental connection between the words and what they refer to. Changing a diaper in the bathroom will also associate the process with the place.

- Although much ado has been made about using the "proper" terminology for body parts and functions, you should use the words that come most easily to you and your child. "Peeing," for example, may be more effective than the term "urinating" if the latter is a forced term. DO use specific terms, though; "going to the bathroom" is too vague. Try not to use words that will make your child think of his or her bodily functions as being dirty or disgusting (for example, "dirty," "stinky," "yucky," etc.).

> **Nothing I try has worked. My 3-year-old understands everything about potty training, but tells me, "I'm not ready, Mommy." So I *try* not to say anything. If he's not ready, he's not ready.**
> *Kyle Lutz, Mill Valley, CA*

- Also help your child learn the meaning of the terms "before" and "after" by using them yourself at the appropriate times.

- Talk about the advantages of being trained: no more diaper rash, no more interruptions for diaper changing, the pleasure of being clean and dry. Discuss training as an important stage of growing up.

> **I don't think there's any one way to toilet train children. They can be tempted, coaxed, yelled at or put on the potty every hour, but they won't really be trained until they decide they're ready.**
> *Marlene Gwiazdon, Osceola, WI*

- Let your child practice lowering and raising training pants sometimes, or putting them on and taking them off.

- Have a potty chair handy on which the child may sit (even with clothes on) perhaps while you are in the bathroom yourself, but only if he or she wants to. The intent is not to get results, but to provide familiarity with the equipment. And let the child flush the toilet for you, to help him or her get used to the noise it makes and avoid possible fear later on.

- Begin reading "potty books" to your child. Several good ones are available. (See p. 73.)

2
Potty Chair, Adapter Seat, or Toilet?

Some experts claim that we complicate the toilet-training process when we require children to learn on several different kinds of equipment in succession. We start them on the potty chair, then move them to the adapter seat, and finally, we move them to the adult toilet.

There is much to be said for using one, two, or all three of these methods. I suspect that the choice really isn't all that significant. Your choice will depend on your child's size, age, and preference; your preference; and the size and number of your bathrooms. Whatever method you settle on will probably work just fine for you and your child.

Potty Chairs

Proponents of the potty chair say it allows a child to be more independent, since a parent doesn't need to lift the child to the toilet. It also allows a child to place his or her feet squarely on the floor when bearing down to eliminate, and the child can also use the support of the chair arms. Because a potty chair is obviously the child's own, he or she will take pride in possessing it.

I know many parents like the flexibility of the potty chair, moving it to various rooms in the house to suit their convenience, and using it for travel as well. (Others claim that a potty chair should remain in the bathroom, so its purpose becomes solely associated with the bathroom.) One disadvantage is that a boy will not be able to urinate standing up—it will be too difficult to aim, and there will be too much splashing.

If the potty chair appeals to you, you should get one before you start training so it becomes a familiar piece of equipment to your child. In fact, you may even let your child shop for the chair with you. You can narrow the choice down to two or three styles, and let your child choose from among those. This can make the child all the more anxious to try it out.

Let your child know that it's okay for now to sit on the potty with clothes on, but when he or she is ready, it will be used as Mommy and Daddy use the toilet.

Choosing a Potty Chair

If you opt for a potty chair, you will probably choose between a miniature version of an adult toilet, and one that looks like a small chair and has a tray similar to those on high chairs. There are some other variations on the market, but these two are the most common.

- Before purchasing a potty chair, check to see how the pot is removed, especially if cleanups are going to be your child's responsibility. If the pot is hard to get out or it has to be tipped, don't buy it.

- Be aware that if you get a potty chair with a tray, lifting it up will be one more step your child will have to master.

- If you want a urine deflector, look for a removable one made of flexible plastic. Potties with deflectors seem to be easier to find than those without them, but if your child is hurt by one when trying to seat himself, he may refuse to use the seat.

- Buy a chair that has rubber tips at the base to prevent sliding, and check the seat for stability.

- Consider buying more than one potty chair, especially if you have more than one bathroom. The extra one can always be used for car travel.

- Look into the possibility of buying an adult camping portable potty for a child who's unusually large.

Cleanup Responsibility

- Make cleaning the potty chair easier by keeping an inch or so of water in the bottom of the pot.

- Consider having your child be responsible for cleanup. Not every parent is comfortable with this, however, and not every child will adapt to it.

> **Potty training is a lot like a first kiss. You can't do much about it—it just happens. In my daughter's case, potty training occurred over a weekend. The key, I found out by accident, was that she didn't want to be taken to her potty and prompted (how silly of me to think that *that* would work!) but rather, characteristically, wanted to *do it herself.* Once we got that straight, all I had to do was praise the results.**
> *Kathe Grooms, St. Paul, MN*

Popular Commercial Potty Chairs

Some of the potty chairs listed below are also manufactured for large companies, using store names. The item is the same; only the label is different.

Century Products
1366 Commerce Drive
Stow, OH 44224

The **Deluxe Toilette Trainer** is made of molded, stainproof plastic. It has a snap-in deflector and a vinyl safety belt. The pot can be removed from the rear. The seat is hinged like an adult toilet seat, but the top section is removable and can become a toilet-seat adapter that fits all standard adult fixtures. A vinyl-coated seat lock protects the adult fixture when the adapter is in place. Suggested retail price: $12.95

In the same style, the **Imperial Musical Toilette** chair is available with an adult-controlled music box that plays "How Dry I Am," with a convenient shut-off key. It comes with a patterned vinyl coverette for the seat lid. Suggested retail price: $19.95

The *Jenny Lind* training chair has a molded plastic finish that looks like wood. It comes with a "security" tray, and also includes a safety strap and a removable deflector. The pot can be removed from the rear. The chair folds for storage. Suggested retail price: $19.95

Cosco/Peterson
2525 State Street
Columbus, IN 47201

The *Less Than a Day*™ toilet trainer is designed to look like an adult toilet. The pot lifts out from the top, the deflector is removable, and the seat plays music only when the child goes in the potty. There is a tissue dispenser on the side. This model comes with a copy of the Azrin/Foxx book, *Toilet Training in Less Than a Day.* Suggested retail price: $26

The *Toilette® Trainer* is a simpler version of the adult look in potty seats. This model's top detaches to become a toilet adapter. The pot can be removed from the rear, and the deflector is removable. This model is available with or without a colorful decoration. Suggested retail price: $12–$13

North States Industries
3650 Fremont Avenue North
Minneapolis, MN 55412

The *Folding Nursery Chair* is a fold-up potty chair with a removable tray and deflector. It has a tip-resistant hardwood leg brace, and the pot slides out from the rear. Available in five styles. Suggested retail price: $10.79–$14.29

Reliance/Protecto
108 Mason Street
Woonsocket, RI 02895

The *Potty Chair* is a basic, molded plastic chair with a pot that lifts out from the top. It comes with a removable deflector and includes a free toilet-training booklet. Suggested retail price: $10.50

Sanitoy/Nursery Needs
140 Sylvan Avenue
Englewood Cliffs, NJ 07632

There are two models of this standard *Training Chair.* Both models (right) are made of molded plastic and have a pot that slides out from the rear. The deflector is removable. One comes with a vinyl chair pad. Suggested retail price: without pad $7–$8; with pad $10

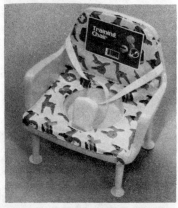

The *Swan Toilet Trainer* and the *Pony Toilet Trainer* (below) are unusual molded trainers shaped like animals. The child straddles the trainer, which does not have arms. The pot slides out from the rear in both models, and there is a cover for the pot when it is not being used. Suggested retail price: $14.95

Glenco
108 Fairway Court
Northvale, NJ 07647

This floor model, called the *Saddle Potty*, is made of molded plastic without a removable pot. It is lightweight and portable, the molded deflector also serving as a handle. Suggested retail price: $4

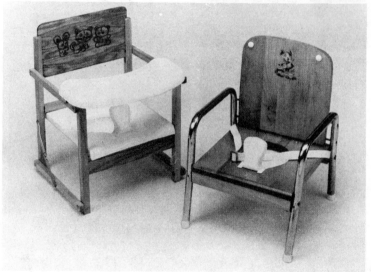

Hedstrom
Bedford, PA 15522

Buster Brown Nursery Chairs® come in two models. Both have removable pots. One has a wooden frame and plastic seat with a removable tray. It folds flat for portability and storage. The second has a tubular steel frame and handles, with a wooden back and seat. The back folds down to convert to a child's step-stool. Suggested retail prices: $15 and $19

The First Years
One Kiddie Drive
Avon, MA 02322

The *Trainer Toilet* has a wide
base with nonslip cushions. The
seat is detachable for use on an
adult toilet. The soft, flexible deflector is removable, and the pot
slides out from the back. It also
has a removable safety belt. Suggested retail price: $14

Welsh Company
1535 South 8th St.
St. Louis, MO 63104

The *Nursery Chair* is made of
yellow molded plastic and has a
safety strap, a flip-up deflector,
and a removable pot that slides
out from the back. The seat section lifts off to fit any standard
toilet. Suggested retail price: $15

As far as toilet training my daughter, I've decided to
leave it up to her (future) husband!
Lyn Souter, Onalaska, WI

Choosing a Toilet Adapter Seat

If you decide to use an adapter seat, be sure to choose a sturdy one that fits your toilet. If you have a nonstandard fixture in your house, most adapter seats will not fit.

Although all these seats seem to come with vinyl straps, I think they're inappropriate. In the early stages of training, the child should not be left alone. No child should be strapped in place and then left! That is likely to feel like punishment to a child. Stay with your child. If you haven't gotten the desired results within five minutes, you aren't going to. As children take on the responsibility of using the toilet with an adapter, they will be on and off by themselves in no time, and the strap is unnecessary.

Adapters are lightweight and portable and have the additional advantage of direct flushing, so there is no extra cleanup necessary. However, adapter seats can be a nuisance for the rest of the family if there is only one bathroom and the adapter is in the way.

You may wish to consider buying a folding adapter seat (purse size when folded) for use when traveling or shopping, regardless of the method you opt for at home.

You should have a sturdy footstool available to help your child get up on the adapter seat. This is also helpful for the child who has learned to use the adult toilet without an adapter seat. And a stool can be of value for a small boy who isn't tall enough to urinate over the edge of the toilet bowl. Quality footstools are expensive but they are a good investment, and you will find many uses for them over the years.

Popular Commercial Adapter Seats

Reliance/Protecto
108 Mason Street
Woonsocket, RI 02895

The molded-plastic *Training Seat* has arms, a strap, and a molded deflector. A free toilet-training booklet is included. Suggested retail price: $4.25

The plastic *Deluxe Trainer Seat* has a pony or duck squeaky top on the deflector. A free toilet-training booklet is included. Suggested retail price: $9.50

The *Seat Ring* adapter comes with a molded deflector. Suggested retail price: $2.50

Practical Parenting
Deephaven, MN 55391

The *Take-Along Potty Seat* is a folding adapter seat made of washable plastic. It fits any standard toilet, and folds to a five-inch square for portability or storage. Price: $5.50 ppd

The First Years
One Kiddie Drive
Avon, MA 02322

The *Trainer Seat* has high arms and a back and fits all adult toilet seats except padded ones. Grip locks hold the seat securely in place, and the soft deflector is removable. Suggested retail price: $8

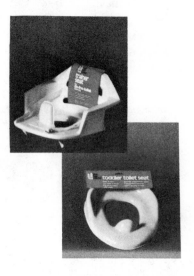

The *Toddler Toilet Seat* is a molded seat with a fixed deflector. Not recommended for padded toilet seats. Suggested retail price: $3

> I know lots of people have used stickers as rewards during toilet training. We let my son choose a sticker and put in on the inside of the lid of the toilet. It worked like a charm, and looks cute, too.
>
> *Susan Boozier, Irvine, CA*

Sanitoy/Nursery Needs
140 Sylvan Avenue
Englewood Cliffs, NJ 07632

The *Comfee Trainer* molded adapter has arms, a safety belt, and a molded fixed deflector. Suggested retail price: $3

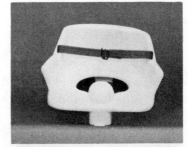

The *Pony Pal Trainer* has arms, a safety belt, and a squeaky deflector head. Suggested retail price: $7–$8

The *Basic Trainer* is a contoured, molded-ring adapter. Suggested retail price: $2

Glenco
108 Fairway Court
Northvale, NJ 07647

The *Jr. Toilet Training* plastic ring adapter has a non-removable deflector. Suggested retail price: $2.50

Direct Use of the Toilet

It is perfectly acceptable to have your child learn to use the toilet without any special equipment. Obviously, the longer you wait to train your child, the bigger he or she will be. An older child is more likely to fit on an adult seat.

The adult toilet can seem like an abyss, and it can be terrifying for a child to sit on it. But certain techniques can minimize the fear and make the child feel secure.

- Teach a boy to urinate sitting down backward on the toilet, straddling it, and pointing his penis downward. If he is distracted while standing, he might forget to aim.

- Teach a little girl to sit sideways or backward on the big toilet.

- Hold your child securely on the edge yourself.

- Teach your boy to aim accurately by having him "sink the battleship." Float the corner of an envelope or a piece of toilet paper in the toilet and have him aim at it.

- Be sure the toilet seat can't fall down on a young boy in these early stages. Have your child check to be sure that the seat is up securely before he urinates.

3
How Do I Begin Toilet Training?

Toilet training is a learning process, not a disciplinary process, and a complicated one at that! Your child has to understand what you want, and then has to learn how to do it. In addition to getting to the bathroom, and getting his or her clothes off, a child must first constrict sphincter muscles to achieve control, and then relax them to eliminate. Obviously there is a lot to learn.

The mastery of skills usually follows a pattern:

First **bowel control,**
then **daytime bladder control,**
and finally (often much later),
nighttime bladder control.

Not every child will follow this pattern, of course. While girls often achieve control before boys, brothers have been known to be dry before same-age sisters. Also, it is not uncommon, especially for boys over the age of 3, to have bladder control but not bowel control. And, of course, there are children who achieve daytime and nighttime control simultaneously.

> My son was potty trained in three days at the age of
> 18 months. I had a potty chair in our bathroom. The
> trick was he *always* mimicked his daddy. (Daddy
> did have to sit down for a while, though!)
> *Rose M. Arndt Kusturin, Knox, IN*

Bowel Control

At some point your child will no longer have bowel movements during the night. They become a daytime process for most children. The more regular your child is, the easier it will be to start bowel-control training. The later you begin the whole training process, the more likely that bowel and bladder control will occur simultaneously.

Explain to your child that you will be taking him or her to the toilet or the potty chair and expect the bowel movement to go there rather than in diapers. Give advance notice about when this procedure will start. Children need to hear what you expect in pleasant tones and words. They can't read your mind.

- If your child has a regular time for a bowel movement, choose that time to take him or her to the bathroom.

- If there is no regular time, try within 30 minutes after a meal. When the stomach is full, the colon is stimulated to empty.

- Consider putting feces into the potty container to show the child where it goes.

- Be prepared to sit with your child to keep him or her company but don't insist your child sit for more than a few minutes—just as long as he or she is comfortable.

- Praise your child for every bowel movement made in the potty or toilet. Also praise a child for sitting and trying to go.

- Since your child will probably still be wearing diapers at this point, you will be involved in getting them on and off. Keep masking tape on hand to refasten disposables.

To Flush or Not to Flush: That Is the Question

It is not unusual for a child to find such satisfaction in passing a bowel movement that he or she wants to keep or to play with the feces and will resist . having them flushed down the toilet. You may need to do the flushing yourself after the child has left the bathroom, especially in beginning toilet training. Other children prefer to wave "bye-bye" and do their own flushing. Having control over the flushing can make it less scary for a fearful child.

While the child who views feces as modeling clay must be corrected, it is best not to refer to them as "dirty" or "yucky." The child may find it hard to forgive you or may feel demoralized by such comments. It may hurt a child to hear that part of his or her body is bad or dirty and is being flushed away for that reason. Explain that feces are the "extra" that your body doesn't need.

Belated Bowel Control

It is not uncommon for boys to achieve bladder control before—sometimes long before—bowel control. Parents sometimes feel that a child with belated bowel control is unwilling, uncooperative, or just plain stubborn, but that's rarely the case. Again, patience is called for.

Constipation is often a factor in belated bowel control. A child who cries, screams, or kicks when urged to use the potty may be doing so because of the discomfort or pain he or she experiences due to constipation. In this case, it is not stubbornness, but fear, that is keeping the child from doing what you ask.

Constipation is *not* diagnosed by frequency of bowel movements, but by the hardness and character of the stool.

The first step in treating constipation is to change the child's diet.

- Decrease milk products (milk, cheese, ice cream, etc.). If a doctor recommends eliminating milk products for any length of time, a calcium supplement will probably be recommended.

- Decrease or eliminate apples, bananas, rice, and gelatin.

- Increase whole-grain breads, cereals, and any other bran foods. Try adding bran to other foods. If your child will only eat bran cereal with milk, and you're trying to cut down on milk, dilute the milk with water first. Offer graham crackers rather than soda crackers.

- Possibly decrease fluid intake (milk, juices, sodas) to increase a child's appetite for bulkier foods. However, remember that fluids are important if you are dealing with constipation and shouldn't be drastically reduced. Encourage your child to drink water.

- Try prunes—the old standby—and dried fruits (if you can get your child to eat them!). Prune juice can be mixed with a small amount of milk. Encourage your child to eat fruits and vegetables with skins on, seeds, and berries.

- Expect to wait two weeks or so before seeing a noticeable change in bowel movements after starting a new diet. Don't resume bowel training until a change occurs.

> I read *more* books while each of my three sat on the potty chair! The books were used as a distraction. It seemed to be useless to say, "Here's the potty, now *go!*"
>
> *Nedra O'Neill, Calumet Park, IL*

Very loose stools can also inhibit bowel control but are often a sign of other problems (infection, milk allergy, etc.) indicating that a physician should be consulted. A diet change may be recommended in this case also, but it should be done in conjunction with medical advice.

> When I was training my daughter, she would do all her business in her training pants until we decided she had to rinse out her own panties.
>
> *Rowena Cook, Anniston, AL*

Daytime Bladder Control

It is easiest to begin toilet training in the summer if this fits your schedule. Summer clothes are light and can be removed quickly. And when accidents do occur, you'll have fewer layers of clothes to launder.

If possible, plan to devote at least three days in a row to begin bladder training. During those days you must be able to drop everything when a child has to "go."

- Tell your child that you expect him or her to tell you if there is a need to go.

- Let your child be in charge of as much of the toilet-training process as possible.

- Put a child on the toilet right after he or she gets up in the morning, before naps, after naps, after meals, after being dry for two hours, and before bedtime.

- Keep your child company rather than strapping him or

her to a toilet seat and going to another part of the house. You might try reading to the child.

- Praise all progress. For some, sitting more than 10 seconds may be progress.

- Turn the water on and let it run for "inspiration," or sprinkle warm water over the child's genitals.

- Ask occasionally if "it's time to try now."

- Set a timer to remind your child when it is time to go potty rather than doing all the reminding yourself.

- Use the reminder as a "before" condition: "After you use the potty, we will . . ."

- Switch from diapers to pants when your child is urinating in the potty several times a day. Better yet, ask your child if he or she wants to try training pants. Be flexible, though, and go back to diapers if they're more convenient for you or if the child wishes to. Some parents like to make the switch in stages, putting pants on a child for a few hours in the morning and gradually extending the time.

- Consolidate success by maintaining the same routine for several weeks.

If you have followed all reasonable steps for some time without success, *stop!* Try again in a few weeks or months.

My son's ability to aim had to be curtailed when he "aimed" over our second-floor balcony into the living room.

Name withheld on request

For Boys Only

- Show a boy how to point his penis down to avoid spraying the room whether sitting down or standing up. (If your little girl wants to urinate standing up, let her try, and explain why it doesn't work.)

- In the summertime, and in the privacy of a backyard or woods, let a boy practice his "aim."

- Let fathers and sons have a "peeing party."

- In the winter, let a boy "write in the snow."

> **At age 3, my son was content to wear one diaper all day long. He was too busy to have it changed or take the time to go to the potty. One day I took away the plastic pants, which meant that he had to have his clothing changed very frequently. He was potty trained in about six hours!**
>
> **Mrs. L. G. Williams, Pineville, NC**

Going Out While "In Training"

- Save yourself worry by putting your child in heavy training pants when you visit. (You'll probably earn points with your hostess, too.)

- Carry a couple of cloth diapers for quick cleanups, and don't forget a plastic bag to store them in.

- Insist that your child visit the bathroom before you leave the house. It will be easier if everyone does so.

- Grin and bear it when (more likely than *if*) your child has an accident in a public place. Most of the adults present will sympathize, having been there themselves.

Dress for Success

- Keep your child pantless or, if this makes you uncomfortable, in loose-fitting underpants with elasticized waistbands. Without diapers, many children are more motivated to go to the toilet on their own. Plastic pants retard "leakage" but they do make a wet diaper feel more comfortable—quite the opposite of the effect you want. Lightweight pants help children associate the idea of elimination with the need to control it.

- Be sure clothing is easy to pull off and on. Avoid buttons, zippers, snaps, and belts during this period.

- Consider attaching Velcro tabs to overalls to make them easy to undo.

- If pull-on pants are too hard to manage, try using a diaper soaker with a Velcro closing.

- Remember that soakers (absorbent, machine-washable wool diaper covers used in place of plastic pants) and heavy cotton training pants shrink. Buy the cotton training pants two to three sizes larger than your child's present size, and wash them before the child wears them. If they are too tight around the legs, they will be difficult to raise and lower.

Nighttime Control

When we expect children to stay dry at night we are asking them to maintain a newly learned mastery of involuntary muscles—while they are *asleep*! This is no easy task. It's best not to make a big deal about nighttime control for a recently daytime-trained child. If you do, the child's anxiety about the problem could delay nighttime dryness for months.

Continue using diapers at night, but praise a child who wakes up dry. Remember that failure to achieve nighttime control is not willful in young children. Developmental readiness for daytime control is not the same as developmental readiness for nighttime dryness.

It should come as no surprise that nighttime bladder control can follow daytime control by anywhere from several months to several years. Maturation is usually what brings it about. There is really very little a parent can do to help a child establish nighttime control, at least until school age is reached.

Be aware that the occasional bed-wetting of preschool and early school years, and even a later return to bed-wetting, are not the same as persistent enuresis. (See p. 64 for further discussion.)

My 2-year-old daughter just couldn't seem to make it through the night consistently without wetting, so we're back to diapers at night only. She was so relieved when I suggested it that I felt foolish for waiting so long. She'll grow to readiness, and in the meantime, it's no big deal!

Penny Dunmire, Avonmore, PA

Helping Your Child, Practically Speaking

- Restrict fluid intake, especially before bedtime. Don't give sweet juices or sodas (especially colas and orange soda, because they contain caffeine), but don't deny a thirsty child a drink of water. Some say that going to bed thirsty just fixes a child's mind on water and increases the chances of nighttime wetting.

- Have your child use the toilet just before climbing into bed. Encourage complete voiding of the bladder or have the child go back to the toilet a second time. Or encourage a child to go twice by directing him or her to void at the beginning of the bedtime process and again, just before lights out.

- Make sure the way to the bathroom is lit, even if only with night-lights. Draw a map with your child showing the way from the bed to the bathroom to help form a visual image.

- Keep the house warm enough so the child won't avoid getting up because it's too cold. You can return to energy saving later.

- Consider keeping a potty chair near your child's bed if that will make things easier.

- Practice "positive imaging" as you put your child to sleep. Have him or her imagine staying dry all night and waking up dry in the morning. Talk about the pleasure of feeling dry, in control, and grown-up.

- Whisper "dry" ideas into the ear of a sleeping child. Psychologists say children are often very receptive to such "idea planting" during certain periods of sleep.

- Let your child know that you know that he or she will stay dry at night "soon," like other big kids do. It is important to set up the expectation, but don't subject your child to heavy pressure.

- Remove diapers and replace them with training pants or soakers only after a week or so of dry nights.

While I was toilet training my daughter, I went into her room several times while she was asleep and gently whispered in her ear, asking her not to wet her bed. To my surprise, she awoke totally dry and eagerly ready to use her potty. For the next two days, I gave her chocolate as a reward for using the potty and continued my nightly suggestions while she slept. Gradually I stopped giving her the chocolate every time, but continued praising her for a job well done. Suddenly, she was trained (both bladder and bowel, day and night) in less than a week. But when I stopped the nighttime suggestions, she started wetting the bed again. I went back to making the suggestions, and gradually tapered off. Some may dispute the validity of this method, but for me, it worked like a charm!

Sherry Weinstein, Scotch Plains, NJ

Keeping Bedding Dry

- Wake your child before you retire and take him or her to the bathroom to urinate. Doing this doesn't necessarily train a child, but it keeps the bed dry for some and leads to nighttime control for others. If your child is almost impossible to wake up, or becomes angry when woken, don't try this method.

- Keep your child in diapers for sleeping. Double diapering may be necessary, or you can line the inside of the diaper with a sanitary napkin for extra absorption.

- Put terry-lined, plastic-covered pants over a toddler-sized disposable diaper to prevent leakage.

- Keep a flannelized rubber sheet, a plastic tablecloth, or a shower curtain between the sheet and the mattress before, during, and for some time after nighttime training.

- Wrap a large terry-cloth beach towel midway around the bed, tuck it in at the sides, and remove it if it gets wet during the night.

- Keep a sleeping bag on hand for a child to finish off a night's sleep if you are not up to changing wet sheets in the middle of the night.

Hygiene

Wiping seems to remain a parental responsibility for quite a while, even after a child has assumed much or all of the other responsibilities associated with toilet training, mainly because it is difficult for children to do a good job. Poor cleanup can be irritating, in more ways than one.

Stress Good Habits from the Beginning

- Impress upon a child that four squares of toilet paper will do the job effectively.

- Teach a child, especially a girl, to wipe from front to back. (Wiping from back to front can cause infections.)

- Insist that hands be washed after using the toilet, and supply pretty hand towels and liquid soap to make the task less boring.

4

What Do the Experts Say?

❦

One thing the experts (it's the *professional* experts we're talking about here) agree on is that you can't toilet train a child until he or she is ready—physically as well as emotionally. Another is that the age of readiness varies widely from child to child.

Most experts, including Benjamin Spock, Frank Caplan, Burton White, and T. Berry Brazelton, recommend waiting for the child to show signs of readiness (usually at 2 or later), and using suggestions instead of pressure during the training process. They advocate rewarding success with generous flattery and praise.

Most of Dr. Spock's advice reflects the conventional wisdom of the day. His recommendation is to use a potty chair rather than a toilet seat adapter, but he admits that it's not a matter of critical importance. Spock also adheres to the idea that the potty should not be emptied by the adult until after the child has left the room. Frank Caplan, of the Princeton Center for Infancy and Early Childhood, leans toward the use of the toilet seat adapter to eliminate the need for the double lesson of first using a potty chair and then learning to use the seat adapter.

Dr. Brazelton's method follows a simple format. First, have your child sit (fully dressed) on a potty chair at least once a day. After that ritual is accepted, undress your child and take him or her to the potty chair. Aim for a time when your child is likely to have a bowel movement, or at least right after he or she has soiled diapers. Praise successes, but don't overdo it. If you feel your child is ready, let him or her play with no clothes on from the waist down, and make it clear that it is the child's responsibility to go to the potty chair when necessary. If your child loses interest and doesn't cooperate, go back to diapers and try again in a few weeks.

A recent toilet-training book that has made enthusiastic converts of some and sparked controversy among others is *Toilet Training in Less Than a Day* by Nathan Azrin, PhD, and Richard Foxx, PhD (Pocket Books, 1974). The program these two psychologists recommend was first devised not for speed, but to help the retarded learn this difficult skill. Later, it was adapted for the average child. Some people feel that the program is overly manipulative and, in some aspects, actually punitive. Others object to the heavy use of sweet drinks and sweet and salty treats.

The demands on both parent and child are considerable. One whole day is to be devoted to training, with no distractions whatsoever. The authors recommend that trainer and trainee be confined to the kitchen, where cleanup is comparatively easy. Here's a brief summary of the procedure:

1. The parent provides a doll that wets and, with prompting from the parent, the child "trains" the doll in the prescribed manner.

2. Liquids are offered constantly, on the theory that the more urine that is produced, the more quickly the training will be accomplished. Salty snacks are given freely, if necessary, to increase appetite for the liquids.

3. The parent is given a sequence of reminders to use, ranging from a firm "go now" to questions about the need to go and general suggestions.

4. The child goes to the potty, pulls down his or her pants (very loose ones are recommended), and sits there for ten minutes, or until urination occurs. The child wipes himself or herself and pulls up his or her pants.

5. Four rewards are given for every success: verbal praise, nonverbal reinforcement (hugs and kisses), something good to eat, and references to "friends who care" ("Grandma will be so pleased"; "Tommy goes in the potty, too").

6. Disapproval is expressed when there's an accident, although "spanking or other physical punishment is probably never justified." The child is then required to "practice" hurrying to the potty from different places in the house ten times (yes, ten!), to feel the pants in order to tell the difference between wet and dry, and finally, to do all the necessary cleanup.

Does it work? Many say it does. And in a formal study of children 20 months to 4 + years of age, Azrin and Foxx found that success was achieved in periods ranging from a half hour to two days, with the average being about four hours.

Responses to a question about the method in a 1983 issue of *Practical Parenting Newsletter* varied:

> "*Toilet Training in Less Than a Day* was our biggest help. (My son was 2 years, 9 months.) The two disadvantages were: 1) it was very boring for me, and 2) you really should stay home for a week to be sure the method has stuck in their brains. Very much worth it."
>
> *Nancy Holte, Cannon Falls, MN*

"Unless your child is eager to please you in general, the boundaries [in this book] are so rigid that you may have a major battle on your hands."

Elaine Whitlock, Northampton, MA

"I have come to the conclusion that when your child is ready, he'll do it. I used TTLD for my first son when he was about 3 years old, *and it worked*! It was wonderful, and I told *everyone* about that book—until I tried with son No. 2, and *it failed miserably*! Now, 7 months later, he's trained, and to this day I still don't know what caused it to happen other than that he was ready, that all the explaining, practicing—not to mention the 'big-boy pants with the trucks on them'—finally clicked, and he understood."

Nance Don, Washington Township, NJ

Using Rewards

Toilet Training in Less Than a Day emphasizes the reward system, which has raised a major concern for parents. Many parents feel strongly that any kind of material reward is wrong or simply inappropriate when a child is learning basic proper behavior. Others don't object at all. And some object only to the use of sweets. The biggest concern of those offering rewards are, "How and when do I stop?" "Will my child expect a treat or gift every time he or she visits the bathroom for weeks . . . months . . . years?"

According to parents who have used the reward system, this is not a problem. It is easy to "run out" of whatever you are using after a few weeks. The kids do accept that. And a reward system can be effective!

Use your imagination for ideas for rewards (you know your children best), and consider combining material rewards with nonmaterial ones. For some children, the most effective

"It Worked for Me"

We used a Potty Box with candy for rewards. A funny side effect was that the other mothers who had been so disapproving of our Potty Box soon noticed that their kids never had "accidents" when visiting us!

Lisa Smith, Hurst, TX

My mother-in-law ordered me to give M&Ms as rewards for correct potty performance. Unfortunately my son responded too well and I (9½ months pregnant at the time) was having to jump up every ten minutes to give him another chocolate and verify that he did the job. I switched to raisins, but he did not like them as much and went back to wetting his training pants. A few months later, he gradually became dry.

Lucy Tierney, Slidell, LA

I think giving candy or little gifts is very wrong. I tacked a calendar to the wall in the bathroom at his eye level. Every time he went potty, he got a star on that day. (I bought those colored stick-on stars.) Some days he only had two stars; other days half a dozen. It worked for us!

Linda Miner, Berkeley, CA

For rewards, we used up two boxes of Life cereal and spent $15 on new books. I think it was cheaper than another few weeks of Pampers.

Susan Ringer, Florence, MS

reward might be calling Grandpa or Grandma to report "success" (this obviously works best if grandparents live within local dialing distance!); for others, it's stickers or stars on a chart or calendar. One child I know was motivated by the promise of wearing a swimsuit all day long if there were no accidents, while a set number of pushes on a swing did the trick for another child.

Material Rewards to Consider

- M&Ms Plain Chocolate Candies
- Jelly beans, chocolate kisses, or other favorite candies
- Sugarless candy or gum
- A sugarless gumball from a toy gumball machine
- Pieces of fruit, crackers, a special cookie, or whatever treat is your child's favorite
- A penny for each "success"—two, perhaps, for a bowel movement
- Big-boy pants or fancy big-girl pants (or a shopping trip to get them)
- Small wrapped presents to choose from, stored in a glass bowl in the bathroom
- Promise of a special treat after attaining a certain number of dry days, be it an ice cream cone or a dollar for spending in the local variety store
- Promise of a really grand gift (a fish, gerbil, special toy, trip to the zoo) after a week or two of continuous success (and then provide it right away!)

5

What If My Already-Trained Child Has Accidents?

Becoming toilet trained is like learning to walk. It happens in fits and starts, two steps forward and one step back. Even among fully trained children, accidents can (and often do) happen. Moments of great excitement or fear, absorption in play, or a bad dream can be the cause of an occasional accident. Illness, stress of any kind, or jealousy of an infant sibling may bring on repeated accidents or even real regression.

Accidents

- Consider the possibility of an undiagnosed illness or an allergic reaction to certain foods or beverages (milk and milk products are often culprits) if your child has repeated unexplained accidents or can't stay dry for two hours. Check with your doctor.

- If your child is ill, expect accidents until he or she has recovered enough to regain control.

- Don't punish a child for an accident. Clean up in a matter-of-fact way, help the child change clothes if necessary, and say no more about it.

- Don't be surprised if your child feels worse than you do about an accident. Your main job might be to console him or her. A child who's anxious to please may agonize over what he or she sees as "shameful" behavior. You might tell your child about one of your own early accidents, if you think it will help.

- Encourage the child to go to the potty after the accident "just to see if there's any more" (there often is).

Deliberate "Accidents"

Most children can't perform at will, but sometimes a child who is able to tries to punish or threaten a parent with this powerful weapon. "Give me _____ or I'll _____," and "Stop talking on the phone or I'll _____" are good attention getters.

- Don't overreact. This is not the time to give the attention that's so desperately desired.

- Do say that the child's *act* disappoints you or makes you angry. (Be sure the child knows you still love him or her.)

- Don't rush to help the child get cleaned up. An already-trained child has learned to be uncomfortable in wet or soiled pants, and a little discomfort now may help to prevent repeat performances.

- Have the child help you clean the floor and rinse out his or her pants, and remember that an *especially* good job of hand-washing will be required afterward. This is not fun!

- Later, be sure your child gets plenty of love and attention, and be generous with praise for every example of good behavior.

Regression

Regression (back to square one!) may seem at first to be simply a series of accidents, but it goes on . . . and on. It's more likely to have an emotional cause than a physical one, and it's most likely to occur during a period of stress: a new baby in the family, a death, separation from a parent. It may last for some time. If there is regression for *any* reason, lack of elimination control will probably be the first symptom.

- If regression is total and lasts more than a week or so, give up and go back to diapers.

- Realize that a jealous child is trying to compete with a new baby on its own level. Play up the boring, unappealing aspects of infancy while stressing the advantages of being older.

- Casually suspend some "big-boy/big-girl" privileges—the later bedtime, some grown-up foods, certain television programs—and show surprise if the child complains. ("Oh, I thought you were a baby.") Do try to spend as much time as possible alone with the child.

- Try to get to the bottom of any other worry you suspect is a cause of regression. Help the child work through grief, or explain a separation in terms the child can understand. Children often suffer from guilt when bad things happen, thinking they are to blame.

- Have the child help you clean up as much as he or she can, but don't shame or scold.

- Go back to toilet training when you think the child is ready for it (he or she may very well tell you), but don't make references to "the first time." This is a fresh start.

- Have someone else take over the major part of the retraining, if possible, to enhance the relief of that fresh start. And *don't* feel like a failure or a bad parent if you do this. In fact, you should be proud of yourself for recognizing a problem and doing something positive about it.

6

Help!
How Can I
Toilet Train My
Uncooperative
Child?

The standard line proffered to the mother of a child who's hard to train is, "No child has gotten on the school bus in a diaper yet." This, of course, is not much help if you are trying to figure out how to proceed.

If your child has progressed from the terrible twos to the formidable fours without showing the slightest interest in the toilet, your concern is justified. If your child prefers to squat, comfortably diapered, in a dark corner, holding a special blanket, you may be dealing with physical or emotional complications, irrational fears, or ingrained habit. You may have a willful child who needs some special handling, or you may be dealing with a simple problem in semantics.

It's also possible that your timing is off. Asychrony is a big word that simply means that a child's "internal clock" is set differently from those of other members of the family. Elim-

Some Questions to Ask Yourself

- Are you determined to have your child toilet trained by a certain age or stage in his or her life, or at some special point in your own?

- Do you see your life as being in a shambles until your child is trained?

- Are you particularly sensitive to pressure from family or friends to "get that child to use the toilet"?

- Do you think your child is punishing you by not cooperating with your training efforts?

- Are you positive that because your child can understand you there's no reason toilet training can't be accomplished easily?

- Have you ever been described as a "controlling" parent?

- Are you strongly opposed to backing off for now and trying again in a month, when all the pieces might fall into place?

ination may not occur when you think it should. For example, a child may have only one bowel movement in two days, or three in one day. If this is the case, it's you who will have to do the adjusting.

And, painful but true, you yourself may be causing the trouble. Ask yourself the questions listed in the box below. If you have two or three "yes" answers, perhaps you should sit back and do a little thinking. Try talking out your problems with your spouse, a friend or neighbor, a doctor, or nurse practitioner—but *don't* take your frustrations out on your child.

One possible solution might be to have someone else take over. Sometimes, for all our good intentions, we are simply too emotionally involved to get the job done. Some parents can't teach their own teenagers to drive, and wisely turn the task over to someone who's better able to deal with it unemotionally. This doesn't mean they're bad parents. In fact, they're to be congratulated for recognizing the problem and taking the proper steps to correct it. It's the same with toilet training. If you can see that the process is getting you too upset, and that you, in turn, are upsetting your child, try to find someone else with some emotional distance who can do it for you. And don't feel guilty! Part of being a good parent is knowing what you can and can't do. You won't prove anything by trying to do the impossible.

Physical Complications

If you suspect that it's a physical problem, have your child checked thoroughly by a physician.

- Consider the possibility of an allergy. Lactose intolerance (the inability to digest milk or milk products) is the most common, but other foods can cause allergies, too.

- Watch for signs of a urinary problem. These include pain or burning sensations while urinating, straining to urinate, color changes in the urine, foul-smelling urine, frequent urination that produces very little or a split stream of urine. Other signs could be abdominal pain or a fever of an undetermined origin.

- Be aware that even after a urinary problem has cleared up, the child may still remember and fear the pain of urinating, and this may complicate potty training. Reassure the child and don't be impatient if it takes him or her a while to get over the fear.

- Remember that diarrhea—persistent runny, loose stools—can cause problems with bowel control. Persistent diarrhea is usually a symptom of a physical problem, and it should be treated by a doctor. It is best not to try to treat it yourself.

- Consider the possibility that constipation is keeping your child from wanting to move his or her bowels, because it is painful. You can help by keeping the child company while he or she is sitting on the toilet, lubricating the anus with Vaseline, or even helping him or her hold the "cheeks" apart to make it easier to move the bowels. Dietary changes can also help (see p. 30). Chronic constipation can put pressure on the bladder and cause daytime, as well as nighttime, accidents.

Emotional Complications

Don't hesitate to seek professional help if you think there's an emotional problem you can't solve. Getting help from a therapist doesn't mean that your child is in serious trouble, and you may find that things improve rapidly after only a session or two. Remember that children often keep silent about fear or shame they're feeling. Therapists are trained to help children learn to express and deal with these feelings.

- Remember that the emotional makeup of a human being is extremely complex. It's not realistic to expect that just because a child is small in stature, he or she will have a small range of emotions. And handling all these strange feelings and sensations is doubly hard for a child because of his or her undeveloped wisdom and lack of information.

- Watch for interference from others. Siblings can set a child off by playing on fears and expectations; friends or even teachers may say the wrong thing.

- Ask your child to show you how he or she would toilet train a doll or stuffed animal. Watch the child's behavior and listen carefully to commands and instructions. If the child uses abusive language, scolds and handles the toy roughly, it might be a clue that your own or someone else's attitudes and actions are at fault.

- Or get the child to draw a picture of a bathroom. Ask for explanations of anything you don't understand. You may get some clues about worries or fears the child has been repressing.

Toilet Fears

Some children—especially those with older, storytelling siblings—believe the toilet is a hiding place for sharks, alligators, or water monsters. The sound of a toilet flushing may serve to confirm this. One mother, on discovering that her child feared the monsters in the toilet, led her child to the bathroom, called the monsters up out of the toilet, and blew them out the window, much to the child's relief.

Don't flush the toilet while the child is still sitting on it. Many children find the noise and action frightening and worry about being "swallowed up." Showing a child how things work inside the toilet tank and taking the child to the basement to explain the workings of the plumbing system may banish this fear.

Willfulness

If you have a truly willful child, you will have seen stubbornness and other signs before now; they don't usually begin to appear just at this time. If you have seen the signs before, look back and remember how you've handled your stubborn child who sometimes digs in his or her heels and refuses to cooperate.

- Consider using reverse psychology: "Oh, I'm sure you won't want to use the potty today; we'll just put the diaper on." Or switch roles: "I need to go potty. Will you keep me company?"

- Avoid "no" answers as much as possible by *telling* your

child it's time to try instead of asking, "Do you have to go?"

- Give choices: "Do you want to help get your pants off and wipe yourself, or should I do it?" "Do you want to use the potty chair today or the big toilet?"

- Physically lead the child to the toilet with a hand on his or her shoulder or arm, not roughly, but firmly enough so the child knows you mean business.

At age 3 my son refuses to have BMs on the potty. He insists on a diaper. I've pinpointed the problem—he just can't "perform" sitting down! On one hand, he becomes very upset if he does go in his pants, but if I suggest he sit on the potty, he insists he "can't." He had no trouble learning to urinate.

Sandra Heath, Brownsville, TX

Comprehension

Intelligent as your child may be, he or she may be missing a piece of the very complicated puzzle you're presenting.

- Examine the words and phrases you're using and ask yourself if your child could be interpreting any of them to mean something other than what you intend.

- Be at eye level with your child while you talk. Use the child's name and have him or her look at you to be sure you have his or her undivided attention.

- Test the child's comprehension by rephrasing your requests and instructions in the simplest language possible.

7

How Can I Toilet Train a Child under Special Circumstances?

Sometimes toilet training must be attempted under conditions that are less than ideal, regardless of our preferences.

You start training a month before the new baby is expected, and then the baby comes three weeks early! Or training is progressing slowly, and you're only halfway there, three days before the family leaves for a long vacation.

You didn't opt for twins, but twins you have—and both are ready and eager to be trained at the same time. Or training has just gotten under way, and Mom gets called for jury duty.

The greatest challenge is probably the one presented to parents of a child who is physically or developmentally handicapped or one who will ultimately be diagnosed as dyslexic. Severe problems such as these will require the advice and cooperation of your physician. He or she will be able to give you information and suggest reading material that will be helpful. Drs. Azrin and Foxx, the authors of *Toilet Training in Less Than a Day,* have worked with those who have disabilities of one kind or another and have also written *Toilet Training for the Retarded* (Research Press, 1973), which is excellent.

The New Baby Syndrome

If you have a choice, you probably won't want to start training a child just before or after the birth of a new baby. Before the birth, you won't be up to the running, and after the birth, you'll probably be too busy. But if you must go ahead with it, think about these things.

- Plan to give the child a great deal of attention. Take no shortcuts. Spend a lot of time alone with the child and do everything you can to set comfort and self-assurance levels as high as possible. (Easy to say, I know.) Involve your spouse or someone else!

- Emphasize the "grown-up" aspects of being toilet trained, and choose whatever status symbols ("grown-up pants," treats) or other rewards you wish.

- Be firm but reasonable. If after two weeks you see few signs of success, postpone toilet training until you're sure your child is ready for it. Do not make the child feel guilty for "failing." (See Regression, p. 49.)

Working Parents

With almost 40 percent of young mothers returning to work after having children, toilet training under day-care providers is becoming increasingly common. Obviously, every caretaker (be it an in-house sitter or someone at a communal center) will have her (or his) own style. Since there is no one magic way to train a child, working parents will need to integrate their system with the one a child is exposed to during the day. If you are comfortable with the general discipline, style, and attitude of the environment your child is exposed to, the odds are you will also be comfortable with the system or process used for toilet training. Group day-care will provide a different dynamic from training one-on-one at home, but the principles are basically the same. One possible advantage of group day care is that peer pressure might speed up the process.

- If it can be arranged, you might take some vacation days to at least get the process started.

- Tell your child's caregivers *before* you start toilet training, and ask them to do likewise. Communication—open, two-way communication—will be extra important during this process. If you both use the same language and have the same attitude toward toilet training, the adjustment from one environment to the other will be much smoother and less confusing for your child.

- Check which kind of potty chair is used at your child's day-care center; it might influence your method of training at home. Also, find out if they use foot stools at the center.

Traveling

Travel may or may not interfere with training. On a short trip, it probably won't; on a longer one, it may. Some children love the idea of a strange toilet, while others will absolutely refuse to use one. And, most frustrating, the same child may demonstrate both attitudes within a couple of months.

- If you anticipate extensive travel, consider opting for the adult toilet seat for toilet training rather than a potty chair. It will simplify your packing.

- Look into the purchase of a folding toilet-seat adapter that can fit into your travel purse. (See page 24.)

- Condition the child to the idea of using a variety of toilets in strange places by letting him or her do just that before your trip. Take the child into gas-station and department-store restrooms; visit bathrooms in friends' homes and in restaurants. If you will be vacationing out-of-doors, demonstrate the "nature-child" method.

- Explain how the bathroom on a train or airplane will look and sound.

- Carry a potty chair or portable camping potty with you on a car trip.

- Or carry a wide-mouth bottle or coffee can for a boy to urinate in. Either can also be used by a girl, if she sits tightly.

- Pack some diapers and plastic pants, just in case your best laid plans go awry.

Toilet Training Twins

Some people say that twins are not usually developmentally ready for toilet training until a little later than singletons are, but others disagree. There's such wide variation among children that the point has little validity anyway. When they're ready, they're ready.

Chances are that identical twins will be ready at about the same time, and here again there are differences of opinion. Some parents try to avoid training them at the same time, holding one off in any way possible, and others believe in plunging in and getting it all over at once.

Fraternal twins may vary as much in readiness as any other two children of the same age, with a boy likely to be ready somewhat later than a girl. Sometimes problems arise with twins when one is both physically and emotionally ready for training and the other is not, but wants (or even demands) to share the experience. If you can manage to train them singly, even months apart, be grateful, and enjoy having just one in diapers.

- If you're training two at the same time, make things as easy as possible on yourself by moving gradually from diapers to training pants. Try pants for just a few hours a day, and when all of you are tired, change to diapers.

- Concentrate on treating the twins as individuals, not as a matched pair. Never compare the progress of one against the other.

I think I deserve a reward for potty training twins. If one of them wasn't running to the bathroom, I was.
Robyn Neuman, Beaver Dam, WI

- Take advantage of the fact that a trained twin will be a perfect role model when the second is ready.

- Supply two potty chairs, in different colors, and assign one very specifically to each twin. It's not reasonable to expect that there won't be times when both have to use the potties at the same time. Allow no switching, or you may have a tantrum on your hands.

Separation from a Parent

If you have been the primary toilet trainer and anticipate being absent during part of the process, you should prepare your child carefully and do some following up while you're gone.

- Suggest to the other parent or whoever will be carrying on the process that this book be required reading; at least mark significant passages.

- Prepare the person who will be in charge with tips and your observations on how best to handle things.

- Explain to the child in simple language that you will be gone for a while, but that everything else will be the same (if it will; do prepare him or her for any changes you know about). Don't make a big deal of the absence. Promise to bring back something special for the child—and then *do* it!

- Try to telephone while you're gone. Casually ask your child if he or she has been going to the toilet as usual. If the answer is yes, express your delight. If the answer is no, tell the child you hope it will be yes the next time you call.

- If your child regresses when you return, don't show disappointment or promote shame. Go back to diapering for a few weeks and then try again.

8

How Can I Deal with Bed-Wetting?

❦

Bed-wetting is considered to be a real problem (it's called enuresis) only after a child is 5 or 6 years old. It may happen occasionally or every night. While it's distressing and frustrating, you should bear in mind that a third of children over 3 and a quarter of those over 4 lack nighttime control. Even by ages 6 to 7, one child in seven is a bed-wetter. Small comfort—but at least you're not alone!

Remind yourself, every time you have to face a wet bed, that no child *wants* to be a bed-wetter. Your child's desire for nighttime control is probably greater than yours. It's been said by many, but it bears repeating: *A child should never be punished for wetting the bed.* Bed-wetting is not deliberate. Nighttime control is largely involuntary. Certain aspects of control can be learned, but it takes time and patience.

Some Possible Causes for Bed-wetting

- Deep sleep, which makes it impossible for many children to respond to body signals.

- Lack of awareness, even in a light sleeper.

- Heredity. If family members have been prone to bed-wetting, a child often is too.

- Being chilled if covers aren't sufficient or are kicked off.

- Stress caused by changes in a child's life or illness.

- Fear of getting up at night, especially if the house is dark and cold.

- Small bladder capacity (a child's bladder *is* smaller than an adult's!).

- Constipation, which can inhibit bladder capacity. (See p. 30 for treatment.)

- Allergy to milk, which may be tested by removing all milk products from the child's diet for several weeks. (A calcium supplement may be recommended by your physician). Other food sensitivities may also be involved.

- Illness (especially if treated with drugs) during which usual nighttime control may be lost and not regained for some time after recovery.

- Sickle-cell anemia, one symptom of which may be inability to stay dry all night. (This disease is present only in black children.)

Helping Your Child, Psychologically Speaking

- Remember that punishing, scolding, and embarrassing a child have been proven *not* to help a child achieve nighttime control.

- Take your child to the doctor for a checkup just in case there's a physical cause for the bed-wetting. This will assure both you and the child that everything possible is being done.

- Be sure to tell your child that you know that he or she is not doing it on purpose, and that the problem doesn't make you love him or her less.

We have four children, all of whom were bed-wetters. Both parents were also bed-wetters. It's a day-to-day struggle, full of restrictions and discipline concerning liquid intake, which made it hard away from home. We persevered, were careful, and did *not* spank—and finally won. Whew! What a relief. (I also had a very dependable washing machine!)

Name withheld on request

- Explain to your child, using simple language, that he or she is experiencing a developmental delay and that there is nothing seriously wrong. This problem is outgrown by 99 percent of the population. (Don't mention that the "cure" often comes with the onset of puberty.)

- Explain to a son that bed-wetting is twice as common in boys than girls and that he is definitely not the only boy with this problem.

- Don't let siblings tease the child.

- Practice positive imaging. Help your child relax at bedtime and imagine waking up dry. This is a form of treatment that doctors are using with much success, especially with children 6 years and older. Or whisper encouraging words to the child while he or she is sleeping. This subtle form of hypnosis can be very effective.

- Offer rewards for nighttime control as you have for daytime toilet training (see Rewards, p. 44). The use of progress charts with stars or check marks is often a helpful motivator. Or ask your child for ideas for rewards.

• Consider professional counseling. Bed-wetting needn't be a sign of emotional problems for therapy to be helpful. Third-party help can simply open up new options.

Dry Dreams

The Institute of Human Development sells a cassette tape that you can play as your child falls asleep. It offers gentle positive reinforcement for waking up to a dry bed, for using the toilet during the night, and for feeling good about this "grown-up" behavior. Write P.O. Box 41165, Cincinnati, OH 45241, and ask for Item BW: "Conquering Bed-wetting," $12.95 ppd.

Practically Speaking

• Work on bladder-stretching exercises. Have your child hold his or her urine during the day as long as possible. Starting and stopping the stream of urine may also increase muscle control.

• Have your child lie down on a bed in a sleeping position and "hold back" as long as possible before urinating. Practice at this will help him or her learn to recognize body signals while lying down.

• Restrict fluid intake before bedtime.

• Be sure the child goes to the bathroom just before going to bed.

• Make sure pajamas are easy to remove.

When Regular Diapers No Longer Fit

When your child outgrows regular diapers but not the need for them, these items can prove helpful.

Pampers now has a Maximum Absorbency Toddler size disposable for children weighing 23 to 35 lbs. **Huggies** also has a Toddler size disposable that fits children 23 lbs and up.

For larger children:

Ambeze Jr. Incontinent Pants are disposable, tape-tab diapers that fit up to a 28" waist. Write:
Whitestone Products
Piscataway, NJ 08854
or call (800) 526-5367 for the dealer nearest you.

The Dry Pride System offers a combination pant and liner as well as a large-size disposable diaper. Write:
Gerber Products
Fremont, MI 49412
or call (800) 253-3078 for a brochure.

Attends is a disposable brief available by the case by mail. Choose the appropriate size according to waist or hip size, whichever is larger. (S) 20"–31", (M) 32"–44", (L) 45"–58". For prices, write to:
Procter and Gamble
Home Service Group
P. O. Box 41713
Cincinnati, OH 45241
or call (800) 543-0400 (operator 708).

- Be sure the way to the bathroom is lit.

- Wake your child up before you go to bed and tell him or her to go to the bathroom.

- Consider buying *A Parent's Guide to Bed-wetting Control* by Nathan Azrin, PhD, and Victoria Besalel, PhD (Pocket Books, 1979). It offers a detailed behavior-modification procedure.

The Battle of the Bedsheets

You can't *make* a child stop wetting the bed at night. Only the child can do it, and then only when the brain is willing. Many parents believe that a bed-wetter can and should be responsible for changing a wet bed and, perhaps, for laundering the sheets. They do this not to embarrass or punish the child, but for practical reasons. It is one way to teach a child that people

are expected to clean up after themselves. At any rate, the process of cleaning up should be made as painless (for you *and* your child) and as efficient as possible.

- Make up a bed with two sets of bedding (including two rubber sheets) so only the top set needs to be stripped during the night.

- Use an old waterproof crib sheet or plastic tablecloth or a large plastic garbage bag to protect the mattress if you don't have rubber sheets or a plastic mattress cover.

- Line the bed with a large bath towel tucked in sideways over a plastic protector. If the bed isn't too wet, the child can simply pull off the towel and go back to sleep.

- Don't forget to protect the pillow with a zippered plastic cover. Kids do move around a lot at night.

- Keep an extra set of pajamas available and keep a plastic laundry basket or plastic bag handy for wet bedding.

Mechanical Devices for Helping the Bed-wetter

In general, mechanical devices, such as moisture-sensitive pads connected to alarms or buzzers, should not be used until a child is 6 years old. The primary principle of alarms is to waken the child while he or she is still urinating. At first, the child probably will not wake up until the bladder is completely emptied. However, as conditioning progresses, he or she will begin to awaken after passing the first few drops.

The disadvantages of the alarms are fairly obvious. The sound may upset the child (though children have been known to sleep through it) and disrupt the household. Older brothers and sisters may wake up, too—the last thing an embarrassed child wants to happen. Alarms have to be reset in the middle of the night, and in hot weather, perspiration can cause the alarm to sound. In cooler weather, the child may get

chilled because the device works best if he or she sleeps without pajama bottoms or underwear.

On the plus side, alarms do seem to have a high success rate,
with reports of 75-85 percent effectiveness in the short term
(from a week to a few months). This is considerably better than
for other methods. However, many families stop using them before success is achieved because they're so annoying.

Cause for Alarm

Alarm devices are available for about $50 through
Sears', Penney's, and Ward's mail-order catalogs.

In addition, two national companies lease
"conditioning devices" for bed-wetters. The fees
they charge may be higher than the purchase prices
of alarm devices, but "counseling" and how-to-use
information are also provided because the
companies feel that proper use is the key to
success. Both companies use behavior modification.
Neither will lease equipment for children under the
age of 4. Contact them for additional information
and the names of representatives near you:

National Enuresis Center
7726 Morgan Ave. South
Minneapolis, MN 55423
(612) 866-7730

Pacific International, LTD
555 Birch St.
Nekoosa, WI 54457
(800) 826-4875
(715) 886-4550 (in Wisconsin)

Drug Therapy for Helping the Bed-wetter

- Be aware that drug therapy can be effective but should be reserved for children past the age of 6. It seems to work for about 60 percent of the children who try it. While the chemical action is unknown, it seems to level off the depth of sleep so that the brain is at a higher level of consciousness. It offers quick results, but once it's stopped, a large percentage of children return to bed-wetting. Drug users need to be closely monitored.

- Be aware that some of the drugs used to treat bed-wetting have side effects. Ask your doctor or pharmacist about the one your child is taking. Imipramine (also known as Tofranil, SK-Pramine, Janimine, Imavate), which is commonly used to treat bed-wetting, can cause personality changes and lethargy. Evaluate the drug after a week or so and weigh its effectiveness against any ill effects it is having on your child.

- Remember that any drug can be lethal in the wrong hands. If you are using a drug to treat your child's bed-wetting, be sure it is stored safely out of the child's reach, and away from siblings too. Children have died from an overdose of these drugs.

- Drugs and alarm devices are sometimes used together to treat enuresis. Again, ask your doctor (or some other professional) and use common sense to help you decide what's best for your child.

- Some parents and professionals discourage the use of these somewhat drastic measures, especially if they are chosen because they're easy. Try to keep the problem in perspective. You and your child should decide for yourselves (with advice from caring professionals) which approach is best for your situation.

9
Books to Read Aloud to Children

Some potty-training books may seem a bit silly to parents, but they're often adored by children because they relate to them so completely. The books demonstrate a developmental step with language and pictures a child can understand, and the characters provide role models. They clearly show what's expected of a child, which we sometimes forget to relay consistently.

For parents, the books are helpful because they take some of the work off our shoulders and provide a point of departure for a casual discussion on the subject with a child.

Some books that many parents have found helpful appear on the following pages.

> **After spending one miserable week being involved with my 2½-year-old's accidents, I simply asked him if he still wanted to be in diapers. He said yes, and so he wore them for a few more weeks. Later, he came to me and said, "Mommy, no more diapers." I am beginning to learn that I do not want the power, not that you can ever have it, over my child's "self."**
> *Mrs. B. Leckart, Los Angeles, CA*

No More Diapers
by J. G. Brooks, MD

Delacorte Press
1 Dag Hammarskjold Plaza
New York, NY 10017 $3.95

This is a two-part book that includes a short preface for parents. Each part presents an illustrated story, one for boys and one for girls, with an appropriate hero and heroine for each. Both stories show the child starting with a potty chair, taking responsibility for emptying it into the toilet, learning to like feeling dry, and being positively reinforced by the parents. While the words "urine" and "bowel movement" are used, the text notes that more familiar words can be substituted if parents wish.

Toddler's Potty Book
by Alida Allison

Price, Stern, Sloan
410 N. LaCienga Blvd.
Los Angeles, CA 90048 $4.95

A "unisex" child is used in this colorful large-format 28-page book. The text is minimal. The art is rather simple, but the cheerful message of feeling good when one is dry is conveyed effectively. Because the emphasis of the book is on being dry, the author manages to avoid the use of any terms for elimination.

Once upon a Potty
by Alona Frankel

Barrons
113 Crossways Pk. Dr.
Woodbury, NY 11797 $3.95

This is a small book with colorful illustrations that are great fun. It is the story of a small boy who is introduced to the potty, has some problems with timing and placement, but ultimately learns to get his "wee-wee" and "poo-poo" in a pot-style potty. The story is a bit silly and may turn some parents off, but it will delight most children.

There is also a companion book featuring a girl. The title is the same; simply chose your book by its cover.

Toilet Learning
by Alison Mack

Little, Brown
34 Beacon Street
Boston, MA 02106 $6.95

This durable paperback is divided into two parts. The first is a parent's guide to preparing yourself and your child for toilet learning. The second part is a colored-picture story that takes your child through the process of elimination, functions of bathroom equipment, examples of all sorts of folks who use the bathroom, the way boys and girls differ in their use of the bathroom, and where we find bathrooms. The terms used for elimination are "wee-wee" and

"doo-doo." However, parents are encouraged to substitute their own words.